Sunshine on a Shoestring

*Reflections on the Joys of Giving,
Receiving, and Living*

by

Almena Smith Springer

Beacon Hill Press of Kansas City
Kansas City, Missouri

Copyright 1981
by Almena Smith Springer

ISBN: 0-8341-0733-3

Printed in the
United States of America

Quotation marked TLB is taken by permission from *The Living Bible,* © 1971 by Tyndale House Publishers, Wheaton, Ill.

Quotations by Bertha Munro are taken by permission from *Truth for Today* (Kansas City: Beacon Hill Press of Kansas City, Copyright 1947.)

All poems not marked otherwise are by the author.

First Foreword

Someone has put it, "All the beautiful sentiments in the world weigh less than a single lovely action." Thus speaks the life and ministry of a beautiful lady by the name of Almena Smith Springer. She, with her husband, unite together in one of the most caring, sharing, sunshine ministries that I have ever known. Together they are alert especially to the birthdays and anniversaries of older people and the arrival of new residents to our community. Almena cooks and bakes and her husband makes the deliveries—and they do it on a shoestring. Not owning an automobile, they walk to the market for their shopping; and Rev. Springer walks throughout our total community, which consists of several square miles, making regular visits to as many as 80-100 each month. It is understandable why they are known and loved as a couple who fulfill their lives and others with "sunshine on a shoestring." How blessed our world would be if their numbers would increase. God bless them!

                        Sam Stearman
                        Minister of Pastoral Care
                        Bethany, Okla.
                        First Church of the Nazarene

Second Foreword

As a little girl I, like most little girls, spent hours stumbling around the attic in my mother's discarded high heels and crepe dresses, feeling sophisticated—if somewhat wobbly in the ankles—and adultly able to meet any challenge. But as I grew to adolescence, it became apparent that simply adorning mother-sized clothes and standing confidently with one hand on my hip did not prepare me for the mysteries and opportunities ahead. I began searching for the models who might be trusted to lead me, sagely but gently, into the world of responsible Christian womanhood.

I was blessed with the presence of two such women in the years that followed. Both were minister's wives. Both displayed an exquisite inward beauty which they wore with humility and gratefulness. Both knew how to laugh—and to cry—at the right times; when to pray, and when a comforting word was sufficient; where it hurt, and why. Their tables were open to all, as were their hearts. My own mother was one of the women. Almena Springer, who has become a sort of cherished second mother, was the second.

It is a gift to me that she asked me to prepare this foreword. I know that any of the scores of people like myself whose lives she has touched deeply would have been equally pleased to have a share in this book. Perhaps it is her sensitivity to the joy I receive from working on my own writings that made her want to share her joy with me in this way; or perhaps it is because I have encouraged her for several years to put some of her thoughts into a book such as this.

At any rate, having been given so splendid a task, I suddenly find myself somewhat at a loss for words. It is impossible to elaborate all of the ways Almena Springer has touched my life during our years of friendship. She emerged as a significant person in my development during those awkward, painful, sometimes exhilarating teen years, and continued to be present to me during college and into young adulthood. She encouraged me during the confusing and promising years while my husband attended medical school, and absorbed each joy and sorrow as one of her own. Every step of the way she responds out of love and has learned that we who receive her love will, in turn, offer ours in her own time of need. She is a rare human being who has discovered fully the secret of being human.

Of the many gifts she gives to people, probably the greatest is her own presence. She seems to have no sense of self-importance, arrives with no pomp or testimony. Almena Springer simply is there with an embrace, a poem she wrote for the occasion, a bowl of corn chowder like her mother taught her to make on Cape Cod, a verse of scripture. She passes by, like a breath of fresh air, and is gone. But one knows when she has been there, and is refreshed.

When she recently moved from an inner-city housing project in Rockford, Ill., nearly the entire community turned out for the farewell party. Her neighbors all wanted to give her something to remember them by, although they had indeed little of their own. They brought what they could, and asked that by these gifts she would know that she was loved and would be missed. Those who read this book and respond, not only to the words but to the spirit in which they are shared, will understand why.

Ruth Bryant Purtilo
Cambridge, Mass.

Acknowledgments

I wish to extend my thanks to several who have helped me in the preparation of this book:
(1) to my young friend *Ruth Purtilo* for compiling materials—and for always bringing out the very best in me;
(2) to my *family* who helped me create the atmosphere for the joy of my homemaking, and to *all* who at some time have been the royalty at my table;
(3) to *Sam Stearman,* my friend and minister of pastoral care at Bethany First Church of the Nazarene; and
(4) to the most precious people of all, *those in the inner city.*

Contents

The Joy of Giving	12
The Joy of Giving Comfort	19
The Joy of Saying, "Thank You"	24
The Joy of Homelife	27
The Joy of Entertaining	35
The Joy of Growing Older	40
The Joy of Christmas	51
Prayers	58

For Helen

Anticipation

I see Him in the tulips
   I planted beneath the snow,
The hyacinth and daffodils—
   What joy to watch them grow.

Beside our picture window
   The pink crab will display
A paradise of beauty;
   Oh, ecstasy of May!

While gentle breeze blows through
   And plays a symphony,
My heart sings, "Hallelujah!
   I know He lives in me."

It's with anticipation
   I wait for it to bloom;
I love to take them to God's house,
   Or brighten up some room.

I think of all the wild flowers, too,
   Untouched by human hand
In places where only God can see—
   How beautiful His plan!

I look up in the heavens,
   The soft clouds taking wing.
And in His plan for making man,
   I see eternal spring.

THE JOY OF GIVING

Though the gift be small and simple,
   If the wish is wide,
Just the simple gift of giving
   Makes you warm inside.

Though the thought is ever-fleeting,
   If a thought at all,
Remember all the mighty big things
   Started out as small.

So if you've a gift worth giving,
   Let it be your smile;
Let it be a kindly word
   That makes the stranger stop awhile.

Let it be a simple gift; then,
   If the wish is wide,
Just the simple gift of giving
   Makes you warm inside.

Author Unknown

A while ago I ran across some four-ounce old-fashioned glass nursing bottles. A rosebud in one for a new mother makes a nice gift to take to the hospital.

While we lived in the Dakotas, I shopped one morning for a birthday gift for a friend who at that time was under an extreme emotional strain. I found in the dime store the most fragile bud vase for $1.00, went to a florist, and bought a red rose for 50 cents. That afternoon my husband delivered it in a blizzard.

Did you know that gifts delivered in unfavorable weather are never forgotten? Or a visit to someone in the hospital as well?

When in doubt for gifts, baked food, fruit, and flowers are always correct. There is so much love in what one has made.

Did you know that in a letter you can include four bags of jasmine tea (or other imported tea bags) folded in foil? or a package of sachet? or pressed flowers from your own backyard? Add your own ideas, there are many. For missionaries, there are Band-aids, needles, Kool-Aid, and many other needed items.

Some years ago I learned to shop for little articles and to lay them aside. Most cost 50 cents or less (I'm afraid inflation has since set in). Examples are little bud vases, candy dishes, notepaper and envelopes. This continual mind to potential gifts helped me to always have a gift on hand when I wished to remember someone and prevented last-minute impulsive buying or the embarrassment of not having the money at the time I wished to give a gift.

I shop as carefully for a card as I do for a gift—I do not like box cards or cards that read, "Sorry you are ill, hurry and get well," or some other prepared message. Personalized cards say so much more with little or no extra effort.

I save all pretty empty boxes (especially little ones), little jars that contained fruit, little medicine bottles, even some vitamin containers (the little apothecary jars). Put little candy hearts or bath salts in them, tie with a ribbon, and some little girl will be delighted. Remember when you were a little girl and had your own room—little bottles were prize possessions! Or float tiny flowers in water in the bottles like miniature rosebuds.

After-Christmas sales are wonderful for finding gifts for the rest of the year. I once found many white frosted candles that were deep red inside. These "Christmas candles" made fine Valentine's Day gifts when presented with a small valentine attached to them!

Belated and extra gifts can be special. Have you ever sent part of a gift at Christmas and held another part so that it would arrive two or three days later as a "special" afterthought?

If you have friends with names like Daisy, Violet, or Rose, "address" a gift or card to them by attaching a picture or bunch of artificial flowers depicting their name. If you sew or embroider, even the simplest gift bearing your "stitches of love" will be a memorable gift.

We can often learn secrets about the joy of giving from gifts we receive. Two examples come to mind:

I once received a box that read, "Do not open until Mother's Day." But the day before Mother's Day my son in California called and asked, "Did you receive the package?" I assured them I did. "OK," my son went on, "Judy is on one line and I am on the other. Open it now." This way they were able to share in the joy of my opening their gift, a beautiful exotic salad bowl. It was a way of bringing us together for this special occasion and enhanced the joy for both of us.

One year the week before Christmas, when I lived in the parsonage and was oh so busy, two trays of cupcakes arrived, 25 of them. Someone had taken time to bake and decorate them. What fun to serve my many tea guests when I was too busy to bake for the holidays!

A gift to make:

Instant Melody Tea

2 c. Tang	1 c. instant lemon tea
2 c. sugar	1 tsp. cinnamon
1 orange rind (I use grated orange rind from the spice counter.)	1 tsp. cloves

Mix ingredients, put in small baby food jars.
Label front: Instant Melody Tea
　　　　　　Use 1-1½ tsp./cup of boiling water.
　　　　　　Made by Heart and Hands.
　　　　　　　Your Name

Cut pictures from a magazine or card of flowers to cover the top of the jar. This makes a delightful gift for tea lovers.

The prayer and purpose of giving (doing good works) is so important! What is back of our giving?

Two thoughts about giving gifts come from Fletcher Spruce.

> Wrap all your gifts in love, perfume them with prayer. [Which reminds me, one *can* perfume some gifts, a delightful touch if done very sparingly!] When you label them, aim to be a blessing. Try to find a way to lift their load.

None of us knows what he accomplishes and what he gives to humanity. That is hidden from us, and shall remain so, though sometimes we are allowed to see just a little of it, so we will not be discouraged.

One tiny violet of encouragement will mean more to those with whom we live today than will acres of orchids when their pulses are stilled with death.

Bertha Munro writes on giving love:

Love is best because it never will wear out. The earthly things we grasp at will give out. Anything that is of the service will die with the rest of the physical, material universe. The heart, the spirit, persons, and their right relationships, will live forever.

Old, feeble, dying, when we can no longer think or work or give, we still can love.

When earth is past and all its knowledge is useless, we still can love. Sad for us if we have never learned how!

A warm loaf of bread wrapped in white paper is a most welcome gift. I put Easter pictures on two tonight and wrote, "Happy Easter, Happy Spring." Sometimes I send one along when my husband goes to visit an old couple. The appreciation is so rewarding. One not too attractive lady in our building who seems never to have callers brought me a hug and kiss and these words, "God is great and God is good."

The lonely and forgotten are so many. Fletcher Spruce reminds us how we should serve them: "Work is not always preceded by love, but love will always be followed by service—His service, for His sheep, by His disciples."

I like this about giving by Henry Ward Beecher:

> Giving is to be with simplicity—there are to be no side-long looks to self interests; no flinging of a gift from a height, as a bone might be flung to a dog; no seeking for gratitude; no ostentation in the gift. Any taint of such mixed motives as these infuses poison into our gifts and makes the taste bitter to the receiver and recoil in hurt upon ourselves. To give with simplicity is to give as God gives.

One who doesn't give the gift he promised is like a cloud blowing over a desert without dropping rain (Prov. 25:14, TLB).

THE JOY OF GIVING COMFORT

He that goeth forth and weepeth, bearing precious seed, shall doubtless come again with rejoicing, bringing his sheaves with him (Ps. 126:6).

See them tumbling down,
Blown by the winds on the ground;
Here on the prairie they're found,
The tumbling tumbleweeds.

Here on the plains I belong;
Deep in my heart is a song.
Harvest will come with the morn,
Sowing the gospel tumbling tumble seeds.

I never say very much at all to a grieving person. I kiss sometimes, my arm about the person; sometimes I say, "I loved your mother [or sister, etc.]." I always sign sympathy cards, "We do care."

Here again, bringing a gift of food or doing some thoughtful act says the most. Do not suggest, "If there is anything I can do to help, let me know"—find or see something to do! There is much work to be done in a home at this time, and the bereaved one is too stunned to think. Maybe you can take a washing or ironing home.

I don't think one should ever stay long when visiting a person in grief unless they request that they would like to have you. "The awesome power of the listening ear" is a gift to be used.

I recall another lesson I have learned about grief: Mothers who lose babies are often never comforted at all, especially if it is a miscarriage. One lady had a history of losing many. I sat beside her in a public gathering and told her, "I do want you to know how badly we feel that you lost your baby." She replied, "Thanks; most people don't even mention it, and you wonder if they care."

The visits really often appreciated are when all is over and most have forgotten.

But above all, the attention of the bereaved should be gently turned to the Great Physician. The hymn writer reminds us, "Earth has no sorrow that heaven cannot heal." Bertha Munro put it this way: "Jesus helps us by being there. Perhaps if you are grieving over much, you have forgotten His presence."

A bitter woman asked her pastor, "Where was God last night when my son was killed?"

The pastor answered, "He was in the same place He was the night *His* Son was killed."

I do not know the author of this, but it has been a part of the real philosophy I've found for my life:

> When all our hopes are gone,
> This know—our hands must keep toiling on
> For others' sake.
> For strength to bear is found in duty done;
> And he is blessed indeed who learns to make
> The joy of others cure his own heartache.

The Answer

With folded hands upon my breast,
Weary of toil and longing for rest—
Rest for the mind and rest from the pain;
Lifted above—some relief from the strain.

Thoughts for tomorrow I dare not weigh,
If I may only have strength for today.
Hours like the ages, they slowly move 'way;
Patient endurance—O Father, I pray.

Where are the days
   When the time seemed to fly—
Skies were so blue,
   The clouds floated by?

Where are the days
   When the heart seemed so light;
Nature still thrilled
   With its coming of night?

When I would waken,
   A new day had dawned;
As I entered the day,
   On my lips was a song.

Then a voice swiftly whispers,
   "O child of My love,
I seek to refine thee
   For heaven above.

"If you would share with Me
   In heaven so bright—
Not all can be sunshine;
   There must be some night."

Signs of Abundance of Rain

Does the present seem just a dark valley,
   The future a mountain of fear?
Are shadows of doubt and suspense
   Around you hovering near?

Life's trials, do you shrink from them,
  Does it seem you've no strength to go through?
You have come to the end of yourself,
  And think there's no more you can do?

Take courage, dear Christian, and listen:
  The showers of blessings He'll send,
For dryness and darkness and shadows
  Are signs of abundance of rain!

THE JOY OF SAYING, "THANK YOU"

It Takes So Little

It takes so little to make us sad—
Just a slightest word or doubted sneer,
Just a scornful smile on some lips held dear,
And our footsteps lag, tho' the goal seemed near,
And we lose the courage and strength we had.
It takes so little to make us sad.

It takes so little to make us glad—
Just a word from one that can understand,
And we finish the task we long had planned,
And we lose the doubt and fear we had.
It takes so little to make us glad!

Author Unknown

Practice being sincerely thoughtful and grateful to people.

If you appreciate something, it is usually for a special reason. Try to express this reason to the person who gave it—describe how you used, where you placed it. You may even find more than one occasion to say, "Thank you."

If you must state, "You shouldn't have

done it," quickly add with enthusiasm, "But I am glad that you did it!"

Some thank-you notes I have received that have warmed my heart:

> ◆ Next to my mom you have probably captured my heart more than any woman that I know. Thank you.
> ◆ The Thanksgiving card was so pretty I used it as a decor at a dinner party.
> ◆ Thank you for the nice Sunday dinner. I love to come to your house, I always feel so loved.

When I lived in the parsonage, I placed little thank-you notes in the bottom of the dish which had contained food—I would also keep on hand little clusters of single artificial flowers and tape one on the dish with the note. I never used the formal thank-you notes—there is occasion for these, I guess, but I did not seem to need them.

I try to write thank-you notes while the expression of my heart is warm. "A word fitly spoken is like apples of gold in pictures of silver" (Prov. 25:11).

Most thank-yous should be sent by mail. *Never, Never* say, "I'll give you this to save postage." Your card loses all meaning the minute you do. If you can't afford postage (and there have been some times I couldn't), then think of some unique way to send it. (If it isn't going through the mail, don't address the envelope formally; it begs for a stamp that way.)

One of my customs, an old one shared by many others, is to keep a dish until I can put something in it before I return it. It tells the owner, "Thank you for sharing, and now I have an opportunity to return the pleasure."

One Sunday while we were at church, our friend Mrs. Daily made us a warm cherry pie, and her daughter delivered it just in time for our dinner. I wanted to express my appreciation in depth, so I came up with this idea:

I taped a picture of cherries from a can into the bottom of the pie dish and returned the dish with a poem—

> Can you bake a cherry pie,
>   Mrs. Daily, Mrs. Daily—
> Can you bake a cherry pie,
>   Cherry lady?
>
> You can bake a cherry pie
>   Quick's a cat can blink its eye,
> And your skill is excelled by no other!

Perhaps your husband received toilet articles, or you have an abundance of toilet water or other toiletries. You can say thank-you with a fine aroma by dabbing a little on a thank-you note or handkerchief.

THE JOY OF HOMELIFE

Growing Old Together (Gracefully)
(A poem to my husband on our anniversary)

I find I must write everything down
From a greeting card to a flannel nightgown;
Then if by chance I send the wrong list—
You may not think that gets me in a fix?

But this is not the least of my lamentation,
For my list goes to Dad, when he goes out today.
"Now be sure to get such and such," I say.
But still my problem is far from solved yet,
For he has nine or ten pockets to get him upset.
To look through them all gets his arms out of socket;
I promise someday I'll sew all but one pocket.

I wait with expectancy, and I hope some grace,
When he walks in with a puzzled look on his face.
"To find that list," he says, "I was not able";
I go to the kitchen—it's there on the table!

On low days—believe me, I have them—I make myself create something. I may bake; and when I do, I leave the bread, pie, or other goodies on a rack in the kitchen. This brings cheer and good smells to the house. Also, someone may drop in for a cup of tea, and the freshly baked goods cheer and refresh your guest. I have many times had someone tell me, "That pie [or cake, or those cookies] was so good I went home and baked some for my family that very afternoon."

Someone has observed that most of the work in the world gets done by people who don't feel like doing it.

Tomorrow is a holiday. I never care for holidays. I suppose it is a carry-over from my days as a child on the Cape when I had a feeling of being very left out of the festivities as I watched others get ready for relatives to come.

Monday is a good day to shop for fruit that is too ripe and is marked down. Last week I took peaches, pears, and apples to make several jars of preserves.

I have been tremendously impressed for years about things people could have that cost either nothing or very little. An example is the public library with its abundance of books, magazines, and other educational materials. We always had lots of them in our living room when I was raising my children. I put them on little tables where the children could sit and read.

Did you know that you can borrow paintings from the library?

Today we went to the park. I brought home a bag of dry pine needles and pinecones, and some stalks of milkweed. A little hair spray will keep the milkweed from blowing free of the pod.

I found a black darning ball with handle at the Salvation Army Store. It is quite a novelty today, but when I was growing up, they got plenty of use.

For some time I've been picking up odds and ends of solid black china dishes. I have enough to use for guests. One does not need to have a whole set, and the plain color goes well with decorations for any season.

At Thanksgiving, for instance, they go beautifully with autumn leaves and orange accessories such as napkins and candles.

And at Halloween I discovered I could use a little black kettle that had contained cheese and use it along with my candles as a centerpiece. They were perfect with the black dishes.

One year in the spring when about to discard my milkweed that had been sprayed with hairspray, I gathered some of the beautiful seeds from the pods and filled a Ball fruit jar (blue) to set in the sun on a windowsill.

Corn Chowder the Way My Mother Used to Make It on the Cape

¼ pound fat salt pork　　1 can cream-style corn
1 medium-size onion　　1 quart water
2 cups diced potatoes　　salt and pepper

Dice salt pork and fry out. I do this in a small frying pan (spider), then slice the onion in the kettle I am going to make my chowder in. Add pork and drippings. Add just enough water to cook onions five minutes. Now add your potatoes and one quart of hot water. Cook until potatoes are done. Add corn and heat to boiling point again. Take from flame, add salt and pepper, dab of butter. It needs to set awhile for flavor. Serves 10.

Nabisco crackers or Pilot crackers go well with this. Of course, oyster and saltines are good too.

Baskets, bought inexpensively at the 5-and-10-cents store, have much potential. I found little oval ones that are usually used for individual baked potatoes—they can be used for many purposes, and they are especially nice for serving snacks.

A little basket with polished crabapples is pretty, next to a vase with branches from the tree. And red polished apples on a counter is not only decorative but inviting to your guests. I have a long oval basket that holds a large bouquet, stems and all, of artificial or freshly picked flowers. The effect is wonderful.

One day I floated a rose in a black sauce dish. It was beautiful. Another time I floated apple blossoms in a black dish, then used my black dishes and pink napkins for an oriental look.

I am knowing the joy now of living only 15 miles from my son, his wife, and our precious little grandson. That we are living so close must be in God's divine will, though we never prayed for it or thought of anything so wonderful.

Grandma has a basket of toys for Paul David and is at last winning his acceptance, although I must admit he warmed up to Grandpa much more quickly and kissed Grandpa on his bald head.

Excerpt from a letter to a young friend: "So we are leaving Tumbleweed parsonage, and I'm afraid, a part of our hearts."

Then an excerpt from Bertha Munro on heart attitude:

> Do not let Satan poison your love for your husband and family with suspicions or resentment. Saint or sinner, he will be yours in the end if you keep on loving; but sooner or later you will lose him and yourself if you stop loving.
>
> Do not ever let your nice words come from the teeth out.

On my kitchen table is an old kerosene lamp that belonged to Grandma Springer. It has blue oil in it—and an Easter lily on one side of it. It's fun to eat by.

Plan one small thing each day to make your home more pleasant. I had a friend who each week had a "Be Kind to" week for one member of her family. Each week there was special emphasis placed on this one person, rotating every week.

Soap wrappers tucked in dresser drawers fill the drawer and its contents with wonderful smells.

Excerpt from a letter to a young friend:

"My very dear friend,

"One of the very first words Jerry ever said was 'home.' When we would come home after evening service, Bob and Bruce in the back and all talking, Jerry lying quietly in my arms, many times I thought him asleep; but as we made that turn into the driveway, he would always hum the word 'home.' I feel like that tonight. My family are at church but at least I'm *home* and 11 days on the road to recovery. This morning my Heavenly Father spoke to me and said, 'These trials [of the past few months] are working for you "a far more exceeding and eternal weight of glory"' (2 Cor. 4:17). That verse had never held any particular meaning to me before, but it became *alive!*"

A letter to our apartment as we were leaving:

"Dear little apartment,

"I am leaving you and, I'm afraid, a part of my heart. These have been three of the most wonderful years of my life; what a heap of living we have done with you. Several hundred loaves of bread have gone from my kitchen oven to say, 'Somebody thinks of you and cares.'

"Home is truly where one makes it and, I might add, what one makes it.

"I don't think there has been here for me what you could call a dull day—ever.

"I pray I may have left an aroma of the spirit of Christ here. I cannot leave all of my heart—there must be some to share with new neighbors and friends I will meet.

"Good-bye, little apartment, and may the ones who follow me be as happy as I have been."

"The future is as bright as the promises of God."

A Tribute to My Darling on This Our 32nd Anniversary

It was thirty-two years ago today
I took to me my darling Almena May.
For those years she's stood with me through thick and thin,
When I know that hers an easier life might have been.

Now in this year of nineteen hundred and sixty-eight
She is yet my wonderful wife and mate.
Though so many times the going has been rough,
You'll not find a woman made of better stuff.

Oh, how nobly she has stood by my side
Since the day I took her for my bride.
Her rewards on earth have been slight,
But rest assured, God the Father will make it right.

Words do fail to fully convey the thought,
To express the full appreciation I ought.
But now let it be widely known,
Though these lines have not shown,
That my heart does throb to fully say,
That I more than ever love Almena May.

Duane Springer

THE JOY OF ENTERTAINING

The Size of Your Heart

(One of Mrs. Springer's favorite poems)

It isn't the size of your house so much
   That matters much at all;
It's the gentle hand, it's the loving touch
   That maketh it great or small.
The friends who come, in the hour they go,
   Who out of your house depart,
Will judge it not in the style you show—
   It's all in the size of your heart.

It isn't the size of your head so much,
   It isn't the wealth you found,
That will make you happy—it's how you touch
   The lives that are all around.
For making money is not so hard—
   To live life well is an art!
How men love you, how men regard,
   Is all in the size of your heart.

Author Unknown

"Be not forgetful to entertain strangers: for thereby some have entertained angels unawares" (Heb. 13:2).

I'd rather have the most simple meal and enjoy my hostess, than a meal with a hostess who is encumbered with so many things that she cannot enjoy her meal or guests.

An Adventuresome but Inexpensive Meal
Grease a 3-pint casserole dish.
Line it with: 1 layer of sliced onions
              1 layer of potatoes
              1 layer of uncooked rice
              1 can of drained peas
              1 layer of uncooked ground beef in small pieces
              1 layer of uncooked carrots (optional)
Pour on top: 1 large can of whole tomatoes
Poke the tomatoes to let the juice go to the bottom, but leave the tomatoes whole on top.
Put a layer of sliced green peppers and maybe one or two strips of bacon on the top.
Bake in 350° oven for about 1½ hours, or until the potatoes and rice are done.
This serves easily eight or more people.

I serve it with just a lettuce salad and hot rolls or muffins. I do my rolls in the morning or even take them from the freezer and wrap them in warm foil.

For dessert—in individual serving dishes, put chunks of pineapple, top these with a spoonful of sour cream, sprinkle with brown sugar, and put a cherry in the middle. This is one of my favorite desserts, light and refreshing.

Prepare everything possible before your guests arrive—I usually do all I can even the day before. When this is in the oven, I clean up the utensils and have time to bathe and take a little rest. Remember, food tastes better to your guests if you do not feel hurried or nervous.

I like to eat with others as well as entertain myself! Haven't you, too, been disappointed when you have been in a friend's home and they confess, "I'd offer you a cup of coffee, but I don't have anything in the house!"

Many times when friends drop in, I make a pot of hot tea and get out my china cups. We have toast with marmalade, or jam, or fresh preserve made the way I used to have it on the Cape.

How to Make a Good Cup of Tea

A heavy porcelain pot is preferable to all others. It should be always thoroughly heated by filling it with boiling water. Put one tea bag or teaspoon of loose tea into the pot and add water that has come to a *vigorous* boil; but water that has boiled too long makes a flat tea. Allow it to stand from one to five minutes. Remove the tea bag.

Variations:
Sprinkle a little clove in while the tea is steeping.
Add ¼ teaspoon grated orange bits with the clove.

Although I could not discover who wrote

these, I want to share them, because they spoke to me when I read them for the first time. I trust that the authors of these words will accept my use of their material in the spirit with which I use it.

The Charm of Tea

Here lies the charm of a cup o' tea:
It warms the heart, it loosens the tongue,
And deepens the smile of old and young.

'Tis not in the tea table daintily spread,
Garnished with roses and thin buttered bread;
'Tis not in the cup, 'tis not in the bowl,
But lies in the sociable flow of the soul.

> My susceptibility to flattery
> Is a disconcerting thing;
> If an enemy but praise my tea,
> I feast him like a king.

> Breathes there a wife with soul so dead
> Who to her husband has never said,
> "This is my own real, homemade bread"?

Breaking bread with friends is one of life's greatest joys. At whatever hour you come, the door is always open.

No relationship in this world ever remains warm and close unless good effort is made on both sides to keep it so.
Eleanor I. Roosevelt

The last quote is a good guide for me in my entertaining. It is more important to please people and not embarrass or correct them than to be able to quote Emily Post by heart. Etiquette is just kindness and consideration for others.

Life's Sweetest Moments

I hope you'll come to have a cookie
   At my house some day.
I hope you'll stay—
   And stay and stay.

We'll chat about our loved ones,
   Our garden and our friends,
Recipes, and patterns; our talk—
   There'll be no end.

And when it's time to say good-bye,
   I'll slip a cookie in
To last the long trip home
   Until we meet again.

Written by Mrs. Springer's close friend, Sylvia

THE JOY OF GROWING OLDER

Opportunity to Look Back

One of the joys of growing older is the opportunity to look back and reflect on past joys. The following poem which appeared in the *Cape Cod Times* is a tribute to the happy days I spent there as a child.

Oh, how well do I remember of
   My childhood on Cape Cod,
And times of poison ivy gotten
   From the cranberry bog.

And then there were the ginger plums—
   How many have you eaten?
Our children may eat "red hots" now,
   But ginger plums can beat them.

In spring we'd catch fresh herring,
   And fry the red roe brown;
And then we had fresh mackerel, too,
   When "Robbin's" cart came around.

In winter, rows of herring,
   Strung on sticks out in the barn,

Were brought to make a tasty meal;
   The bones caused no alarm!

Our cellar was the supermarket.
   Though small, yet it would hold
Enough food to feed our family
   Through winter long and cold.

And then there was the grocery cart
   From J. O. Hulse's store;
Twice a week he'd make his rounds
   If we needed any more.

Oh, yes—there was the sweet fern
   From which my dad made tea
That we were often made to drink;
   We had no doctor's fee.

I must not forget the eels
   That Dad caught through the ice;
Even though they looked like snakes
   They tasted mighty nice!

Saturday night in every home
   Was such a gala affair;
Everybody took a bath
   And changed his underwear.

And then there was the Sabbath day
   That made my heart so glad.
I thank God for the old-time religion,
   The type that my folks had.

Another poem about Cape Cod—printed in the *Cape Cod Times.*

May Flowers

April showers bring May flowers,
   Harbingers of spring;
These tiny, dainty little flowers
   Such reminiscing bring.

Meadows filled with buttercups,
   Golden as the sun,
Standing tall and stately,
   The blossoms tiny ones.

Fields of daisies all abloom
   Will have you in their spell;
How many petals have I plucked
   To see if daisies tell?

Walking through a wooded lot—
   Oh, what a peace of mind!
What lady slippers here and there
   At the feet of fragrant pine.

If I could go across the miles
   To these wild flowers of beauty,
My happiness would know no bounds,
   My journey not be futile.

Flowers of exotic bloom
   Some may long to see,
But give me only wild flowers
   On Cape Cod by the Sea.

There are such tremendous possibilities in trying to cultivate one's personality. I started so late in life. There is a book entitled *Practicing the Presence of God*. Why not practice the fruits of the Spirit and try one each week!

As I have grown older, I have become increasingly aware that there is a real gift in learning to do ordinary things in an extraordinary way. One can cultivate a personality so that people will remember things about you. Along with practicing some fruits, I also am trying to keep my voice soft and warm, not excitable unless over some happy event. I have to try to remember to walk across the street to tell my neighbor something; it's so easy to take on others' habits!

Bertha Munro wrote:
With time we become like the God we worship. If our God is love we become loving and kind; if we spend our lives serving money we become hard and metallic.

We cannot be both!!

Each period of life offers opportunity to make a contribution impossible at any other period. In youth we offer our ardency to God and others. In approaching age we shall offer our poise, our experience, our sympathy. Qualities which it was impossible to offer at any other age. To grow old, not only gracefully but gratefully is the Christian's privilege.

I place my hand in God's today. He puts purpose and meaning into every stage of life. We make a mistake when we try to become self-made men or women.

A gracious woman retaineth honor: an excellence; characteristic attraction; an endowment, natural or acquired; elegance of action or language.

Some people go to schools of culture, but all they acquire is the *shell* of culture.

A Retirement Ministry in the Inner City

Since Rev. Springer's retirement from the ministry in 1969, he and his wife have lived in a housing development in a large Illinois town. Rev. Springer has a large and successful ministry in the Home Department of the church they attend. Mrs. Springer's ministry among the members of the community where they live is described in part from excerpts of letters to friends. The excerpts are included below.

"I would like to describe my life here in the court, but I hardly know where to begin. Let me give you an example of some of my neighbors as a start: My next-door neighbor is a young woman with six children, the youngest not yet in school. Her husband just disappeared one day when she was pregnant with her last child and has never been seen since. Next door to her is a young couple with four children. One night recently her little girl fell on an old garbage can and cut her leg. I had to call the police car (many here do not have cars). When anything like this happens, a whole line of people gather, seemingly out of nowhere, and tonight was no exception. I took the girl into the house and closed the door.... The crowd outside vanished as quickly as they had appeared. I should mention that the young couple is mute.

"On the other side of me is the mute woman's mother. The old mother seems never to have any company except the mute daughter. One day I took her some cookies and she patted me and said, 'God bless you, I don't know hardly anyone here, but I live near my daughter to help her, because she was born that way.'"

"I try to keep Band-Aids on hand, a good supply. Children often come to the door when they have stepped on a rusty nail and ask me to put a Band-Aid on it...

"I've loaned (without expecting to ever get them back) many things. The funniest was a roll of toilet tissue, really early one morning. I think they come for aspirins more than anything else. Some folks probably think I'm crazy for doing this, but I wouldn't have missed some of the rewards for anything. When the children's mute dad had a birthday, they sent me some birthday cake! ... That's just one example."

"There is an addendum to the story I told of the little girl who cut her hand. I must have spent an hour with them; and when I returned home, I sat down on the davenport with another neighbor lady and sighed, 'Well, that's excitement enough for one evening!' She agreed, but in a few minutes she had an epileptic seizure. It scared me; I was afraid she would hurt herself, but fortunately she didn't."

"The one great temptation here is to gossip. One see so much and gets so disgusted sometimes. . . . I've had to ask the Lord for strength many times."

"We hold church services here each Sunday in our community building. My husband has charge, and we have four preachers in this area who preach."

"As I started this page, an elderly lady came to the door. She was crying and asked if I'd keep her bankbook and her money for her. . . . She was going away and had locked her door but had received a call earlier which frightened her. A man said he was from the bank and that there was an error in her savings account. He said he'd be out to the house to straighten it up. After a while she decided to let me call the bank; and the man told me that of course, no call like that came from them. He asked me to keep her with me, and in a few minutes two private detectives were here. They said she did the right thing.... There is so much of this kind of thing going on here."

"I know I need prayers for health and strength to carry on here. But it grows upon me that I want to carry more than *cheer*. I want to carry, too, a loaf of bread, cookies, etc. to these people. I want to walk so close to Him that they will see Christ in me."

"Conditions have not been very favorable for me to even tear myself away and try to write. I *should* write down the events of each day here. There have been seven robberies right around us in the past few weeks... One was so close you could stand at your door and spit on her doorstep (that is if you weren't a lady and knew how to spit!). Saturday we had a lovely, private wedding: the daughter of a neighbor who lives in here. That evening another neighbor, a young man 23 years old, was shot and killed in a bar. The bullet was not intended for him. He left a little wife 18 years old who has been having therapy for a stroke."

"I love living here . . . I have never been happier. The Lord has given me good health for a woman who is 60. I actually feel younger than I did years ago. I can walk long distances now, and I work harder than I ever have. God has given me the hearts of many people. Some women, so profane and appearing so 'hard,' hug and kiss me and tell me how they love me.

They often ask me to pray with them. I am learning so much about life and so fast! Don't ever think life ends at some particular age!!"

"Last week I was interviewed by five different security people. There have been five robberies right around me, one man molesting children, and to top it off two white women in a fight ended up rolling on the ground with one biting the other. There was so much commotion that it ended up with 10 policemen surrounding the area, some with rifles on their shoulders. (I'd only seen this on TV before.)"

"Couldn't you come to visit me? You need to see this way of life to add to your many rich experiences."

"One should set goals for every year of one's life. Age makes no difference—your goals may be of a different nature."

"Look for rich experiences out of the everyday. Breathe a prayer that the day will hold a bright spot for these who need it. Better still, you make that bright spot!"

It is 7:30. While waiting for some bacon to warm, I called my 91-year-old neighbor who is living alone and back from the hospital. She suffered a broken back and ankle. I called because her only daughter has cancer (her mother doesn't know it). I thought maybe they needed my husband's help. Up the street one house is another neighbor. Mr. Springer took her out of town to the hospital yesterday, then went back in the evening and got her. Her husband has had 60 percent of his stomach removed. They are both around 70.

Upstairs are my dear friends Mrs. Daily and her maidenly daughter. Mrs. Daily went to the hospital Sunday morning (she's 88) and is not doing too well. Her daughter is so devoted to her—Mrs. Daily would otherwise have been in a nursing home long ago. I pray for wisdom for words to comfort and help. Here's where I really think actions speak the loudest.

When my 91-year-old friend asks me, "Did I tell you the story..." I reply, "Yes, I think you did, but tell it again, it was so good!" Her eyes shine, and she tells it with such a sense of humor.

The capital joy of growing older is the accumulation of lifelong friendships.

Though the long vistas of a dead past arise
To hide the misty beauty of your eyes;
Though years may spread their mighty wings
    between
And e'en though darkening death shall part us
    twain;
I know that sometime, somewhere, we shall
meet again—And you
will find me true!

Author Unknown

Friends

Praise.
Deliver bouquets.
Remember to forget
   failures and weaknesses.

Correspond.
Share experiences.
Regret delayed answers
   when duties press.

Yearn
As time passes
   to
Sit down to a
   cup of tea.

Written by Mrs. Springer's close friend, Sylvia

THE JOY OF CHRISTMAS

Christmas Reminiscences

Once again it's Christmas,
   The happiest time of the year;
And I start reminiscing
   Of memories most dear.

We've lived in many places,
   And spent the holidays,
So for just a little while
   On some of these I'll gaze.

It seems that old New England
   And Cape Cod's long arm
To the Christmas of my childhood
   Lends a special charm.

There was Christmas in New Hampshire
   When I was just a bride,
An inexperienced preacher's wife,
   And many things beside.

Then Christmas in Lake Placid
   Is so beautiful to see—
Snow blankets the sleeping ground
   And decorates each tree.

We moved to Minnesota—
   This is my husband's state.
I now shared in his family—
   His relatives were great.

Our next move was North Dakota.
   I learned to love the place,
Tho' I was often homesick
   For the mountains, trees, and lake.

We then moved to Wisconsin;
   And though the stay was short,
It leaves with us some memories
   Of friends we loved a lot.

Back to North Dakota—
   We feel like natives now;
For 14 years we've lived here—
   We've wrinkles on our brow.

The miles, they separate us,
   And they would bid us stay;
But hearts go home if feet cannot
   When it is Christmas Day.

A Christmas Letter

Dear Friends:
   "Happiness is awakening at 5:30 a.m. The house is still and dark—having no special form of prayer—sometimes the sentences are as sim-

ple as 'Help me' or 'Thank You' or just listening to what He has to say.

"Happiness is rising between six and seven while the house is still quiet, going to the picture window to pull back the drapes and drink in the colorful sky, hearing the scraping of my husband's snow shovel. I snap on the outdoor Christmas lights.

"Happiness is the awareness of living in the parsonage where a long row of gleaming icicles reach almost to the bottom of the kitchen window.

"Happiness is the tall, spreading Norway pine that doesn't touch the ceiling but almost, brought by your son who is home and a senior this year.

"Happiness is a grandson who likes your molasses cookies—special ones, you know, like you used to give to his dad—frosted with peppermint; and as he eats it, he lightly trips around and almost dances, looking so happy, while the crumbs fall around his toes.

"Happiness is planting a flower garden on Christmas Eve—dahlias, calendulas, and marigolds—then putting them in the little greenhouse sent by your son and daughter-in-law in California.

"Happiness is receiving a pair of pillow slips with crocheted lace from Grandma Springer, who is now 86. You remind yourself you will only use these for special occasions, as you want them to last a long time.

"Happiness is a silver-sealed dragon with jaws flaming red, that sits at Dad's elbow and toasts his bread; he hands it fat slices, and one by one the dragon hands them back—a beautiful toaster.

"Yes, happiness is many simple things; a plain, clean room; the shelter of roof above my head; wet roofs beneath the lamplight; raindrops in the flower cups; the cool kindliness of sheets; a cup of tea with dear and gracious friends; the laughter of a little child.

"May your happiness abound this year."

(More on Happiness)
Another, More Recent, Christmas Letter
Dear Friends:
"Happiness is getting up early and watching God make a day.

"Happiness is living next door to people with all kinds of needs and problems, and feeling that you are living in a very special place—where people come when weary, gay, sad, needing to borrow; where the latch is always open.

"Happiness is sharing ourselves and what we have with others or giving ourselves away.

"Happiness is wild flowers that my husband brings me when he walks long trails into wooded paths—Queen Anne's Lace, Wild Baby Breath, from which to make airy bouquets.

"Happiness is watching little sparrows in the tree—in the gloom of a winter blizzard—hanging upside down from a wind-tossed twig, twitching at the food you put on the twig.

"Happiness is little children filled with wonder and delight—the tender kiss of a grandchild; waiting to see one of yours for the first time at Christmas.

"Happiness is footpaths to coffee klatch, walking with friends, kindred feelings.

"Happiness is the fragrance of a rose, church chimes ringing, frosty icicles, a lighted candle quietly giving its life away.

"Happiness is walking by the seashore, the sea in all its moods, a thick white fog in the air, bayberry candles, piney scents, faces of old friends.

"Happiness is above all having a personal encounter with the Christ of Christmas.

"May your happiness abound this Christmas."

A Christmas Poem

Mary, chosen vessel, to give our Savior birth;
Lovely Jewish maiden, creature of the earth.
Mary, to be mother of the Son of God—
Oh, to miss this honor you could ill afford.

Mary, it was from you He took on humanity,
And from the very God himself He got His
  deity.
Mary, what an honor to rock His little bed,
Bathe, love, and cherish Him and from your
  breast be fed.

And as He grew in wisdom and favor with the
  Lord,
Yours it was to train Him and point His heart to
  God.
Mary, chosen vessel, how I wonder if you knew
That in giving Him to others He's become
  your Savior too.

Christmas, 1964

Prophecy Fulfilled

Four hundred years before His birth,
Ere in the flesh Christ came to earth,
A man of prophecy foretold
What Scriptures to us now unfold.

"To you," he said, "a Child is born
Who comes to earth from gloried throne.
To you a holy Child is giv'n,
God's Gift to you sent down from heav'n.

"Wonderful and everlasting He,
A Counselor for you and me,

The mighty God and Prince of Peace;
His government shall never cease."

And so today, Christ is to me
All that the prophets said He'd be.
I never can express it well;
'Tis more than human tongue can tell.

Conquest magazine
December, 1953

PRAYERS

I'm a pilgrim and a stranger;
   This is temporary land.
On my journey to the future
   God has made for me a plan,
In this land of transient beauty
   Held me carefully today,
Holding lightly, never grasping
   Things that soon shall pass away.

Help me, Lord, for Thee to witness,
   Tell to other travelers too
Of a future that is brighter
   Than the heavens above are blue.
Let my eyes be fixed on Jesus;
   Cause my feet no more to roam.
Clouds of witnesses surround me;
   I will find my pathway home.

There my pathway will be sunshine,
   Not a tear to dim the eye.
Earthly cares I'll leave behind me,
   There will vanish every sigh.
No more heartaches, no more sorrow,
   And we'll never say, Good-bye.

When I step from earth to glory,

He will take me by the hand,
Lead me to my heavenly mansion
Built by Him and not by man.
I will shout thro' heaven's portals—
Angels echo back the strain—
"Glory, glory, hallelujah;
Glory, glory—praise His name."

A Prayer for Guidance

(I place my hand in God's today)

Are there invitations or gifts that should be acknowledged—is there someone sick, a gift of food or a telephone call to make? Who deserves a word of praise or comfort? Should some borrowed or empty dishes be returned?

Love is now—I must not let a day go by without doing some good deed of kindness—and if any reward comes, I must give that away too. Almost always I have felt the deed done in the morning is most effective and my day more rewarding.

A Prayer for the Budget

I do not ask to choose my path; in all my seeking for help and comfort, the arm of flesh falls far short. I plunge myself upon Thy mercy;

may I touch the hem of Thy garment today. May love be predominant in my life to all.

The budget will be small this week; help me to prepare my heart and hands for this.

I have used all Thou hast put into my hands for Thy glory—the only bank account or saving that I have, Lord, is Thee.

Touch my budget, Lord, until I'll be able to do not only for my family but, even as the little lad's lunch on the mountainside, there will be some left over for others.

A Prayer

Have You ever felt like the lights were all gone out? All the beautiful stars in Your sky didn't shine any longer—did giving Your Son put them all out for You? Could all the love You were to receive later in redeeming mankind compensate for the loss of Your Son for the time being? Yes, I know there was the afterward—was it ever hard for You to wait for that? I read recently that sorrow comes to stretch out space in the heart for joy—was that true for You? Did stretching Your heart make You feel— oh, so empty?

Did having Your Son back make all the stars light up again? Did it make every little thing that You did take on meaning and purpose again? Why did You have to suffer so? Is it true that sometimes the thing our life misses helps more than the things that it gets?

How did You go about getting Your broken heart mended? Did just one person, Your Son, bring all this about? Why is it that just one person can do so much to make one sad or glad? Why can such little things hurt or help so? Why not just big things?

Sometimes when You look on mankind, does all seem right with the world? Do You laugh, and do Your feet feel light as You run upon errands of mercy? Do You have other days when so many things seem wrong, and Your feet feel heavy and You don't run, that You don't get as many errands done on those days?

Do You smile as You see me on both kinds of days like this? Is it possible that in the dark days I'm really getting the most accomplished? I wonder. Do You make the joy of others cure Your own heartaches? Are You successful all the time in doing this?

Thanks for identifying with me—it helps, and especially so today.

A Prayer in the Morning

Our Father:

As I draw closer to Thee this morning, a beautiful cool breeze blows in from my window casing. The birds have been already singing a long time. May I come into Thy presence with singing and praise.

Thank You, dear Father, for the night's rest and rain and cool breeze that broke the sultry night, and now for a brand-new day Thou hast given to me.

I need Thee, Lord, today—Thy help and grace, that first of all I may be a blessing right here in my home.

May my life's words and deeds be helpful to these in my own household today. May I give them cheer, courage, and humor.

Prayers on Sunday Morning

Dear Lord:

This day belongs to Thee, and I am only a steward of it. In a sense it will be pretty much as I choose to make it. In another sense I do not have control over it: Tragedy, sorrow, discomfort, and of course, some wonderful things too, may come—all of which could change the whole pattern of my living. Again my responsibility is to react and prove my trust and faith in Thee.

What a privilege to go to Thy house and with others worship Thee. May I go this Sunday with an open heart and mind to receive the truths Thou hast for me. But may I not go alone for the help I receive, but may I radiate the fruits of the Spirit that I also may be a blessing to others.

This is the day that the Lord hath made. Help me to rejoice and be glad in it.

Our Father:

We thank Thee that Thou hast brought us safely to another Lord's day. Help us as we prepare to go to Thy house of worship today. Though our attire may not be as nice as some, let it be clean and attractive. May we lift our heads high and wear it as the crown that Thou hast given us. Above all, may our hearts be right in Thy sight. May we go gladly into Thy house, with a prayer on our lips.

As we sing, let praises come from our hearts; and even as the throat of the little bird throbs, may we for whom He has much more care throb with the wonder that Jesus found us.

Our table has not been heavily laden this week, but we have not been hungry. So as we place our tithe and offerings in service and worship to Thee, help us to know that using it upon ourselves would have brought no gain but only leanness to both body and soul. So let us give with cheerful hearts, in a state of joy, for Thou dost love a cheerful giver.

We thank Thee that Thou hast chosen the

foolishness of preaching to bring salvation to men. May we listen, that through the voice of Thy servant we may hear Thee speak to our hearts.

                In Jesus' name,
                Amen